MAKERSPACE SURVIV

MAKE IT OUT ALIVE
IN THE
ARCTIC AND
ANTARCTIC

Claudia Martin

PowerKiDS press.
New York

Published in 2018 by The Rosen Publishing Group
29 East 21st Street, New York, NY 10010

Produced for Rosen by Calcium
Editors: Sarah Eason and Jennifer Sanderson
Designer: Emma DeBanks
Picture Research: Rachel Blount
Illustrator: Venetia Dean

Picture credits: Cover: Shutterstock: Igor Kovalchuk (br), Shaiith (bg). Inside: Shutterstock: Avatar_023 14,
Axily 14–15, DejaVuDesigns 22, Maksym Deliyergiyev 7, DonLand 37t, FloridaStock 42, FotoRequest 34,
Volodymyr Goinyk 36–37, Gontar 29, Arina P Habich 23, Incredible Arctic 40–41, Ivancreative 5c, Marcel
Jancovic 38, Hayati Kayhan 5t, Kzww 26, Jonathan Lingel 31, Dmytro Lobodenko 32, Madlen 47, Mady70 8,
Nataliia Makarova 24, MP cz 13, Tyler Olson 44, Outdoorsman 27, Pavel L Photo and Video 16, Nick Pecker
28, Pegasusa012 6, Grigorii Pisotsckii 20, Ondrej Prosicky 11, Dmytro Pylypenko 4, 35, Vova Shevchuk 25,
VPales 12, Zbindere 18–19; Wikimedia Commons: Henry Bowers (1883–1912) 30, Butorin 10, Edward S.
Curtis 9, NASA/Lora Koenig 39, Felix Riess 40b, Rolf Steinmann 18.

Cataloging-in-Publication Data
Names: Martin, Claudia.
Title: Make it out alive in the arctic and antarctic / Claudia Martin.
Description: New York : PowerKids Press, 2018. | Series: Makerspace survival | Includes index.
Identifiers: ISBN 9781499434750 (pbk.) | ISBN 9781499434699 (library bound) | ISBN 9781499434576
  (6 pack)
Subjects: LCSH: Wilderness survival--Polar regions--Juvenile literature. | Wilderness survival--
  Juvenile literature.
Classification: LCC GV200.5 M35 2018 | DDC 613.69--dc23

Manufactured in China.

CPSIA Compliance Information: Batch BS17PK: For Further Information contact Rosen Publishing, New York, New York at 1-800-237-9932

Please note that the publisher **does not**
suggest readers carry out any practical
application of the Can You Make It?
activities and any other survival
activities in this book.

A note about measurements:
Measurements are given in U.S.
form with metric in parentheses.
The metric conversion is rounded
to make it easier to measure.

CONTENTS

CHAPTER 1
SURVIVE THE ARCTIC AND ANTARCTIC

You are about to be airlifted onto the ice, somewhere near the North or South Pole. Completely alone, you must find your way to a human **settlement**. To make your mission even more difficult, you cannot take any food, drink, or a tent.

Will You Make It Out Alive?

We are leaving you with one vital piece of equipment: a camping stove with liquid fuel to burn in it. Without it, you would have no chance of survival. You can dress in your choice of clothing and footwear. Apart from these essentials, you must provide yourself with food, drinking water, and shelter by making your own equipment. You are allowed to use any local materials you can pick up along the way. We are also providing you with a backpack in which you will find some interesting materials and tools.

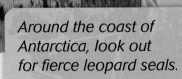

Around the coast of Antarctica, look out for fierce leopard seals.

4

What Is in Your Backpack?

The following materials and tools are in your backpack. When you come across a "Can You Make It?" activity in this book, you must choose from these items to construct it. Each material can be used only once. Study the list carefully before you set off. You can find the correct solutions for all the activities on page 45.

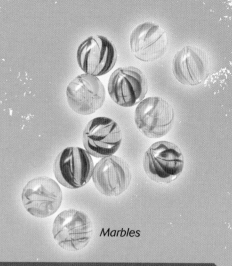
Marbles

Can You Make It?

Materials
- 2 emergency blankets
- 4 metal poles, each 4 feet (1 m) long
- 6 garden stakes
- 6 metal buckets
- Aluminum foil
- Cord, 7 feet (2 m) long
- Thread
- Cotton balls
- Fake fur, 20 x 20 inches (51 x 51 cm)
- Inflatable mattress
- Marbles
- Paper towels
- Plastic bottle
- Plastic bubble wrap
- Plastic headband
- Polyester fiber stuffing
- Sewing needle
- Tape
- Tarp, 10 x 10 feet (3 x 3 m)
- Wire, 200 feet (61 m) long

Tools
- Glue gun
- Pair of scissors

Sewing needle

Survival Tip
Use the Internet to look up all the items in your backpack before you begin your journey. Make sure that you understand what they are and how you might be able to use them.

5

THE POLES

Before you set off on your polar expedition, find out about the environment you will be facing. At the poles, it is freezing cold because the sun never rises high in the sky.

The Ends of Earth

The Arctic is the region north of the Arctic Circle that is at around 66 degrees north **latitude**. North of this line, the sun is above the horizon for 24 hours of the day on at least one day during summer (known as the midnight sun). It is below the horizon for 24 hours on at least one day in winter. This is also true in the Antarctic, south of the Antarctic Circle. This **phenomenon** is caused by Earth's tilt, which points the northern **hemisphere** toward the sun for six months of the year, while the southern hemisphere is pointed away.

The North Pole (above left) is in the middle of the Arctic Ocean. The South Pole (above right) lies in the continent of Antarctica.

Ice and Snow

At the North Pole, in the middle of the Arctic Ocean, the temperature averages -4° F (-20° C). The sea here is always covered by ice about 8 feet (2.5 m) thick. In winter, the sea ice stretches for 5 million square miles (13 million sq km), but much of it melts in the summer. The northern tips of Alaska, Canada, Finland, Iceland, Norway, Russia, and Sweden lie in the Arctic Circle, along with several islands. This land is **tundra**, a habitat covered by snow in winter. In the summer, mosses, grasses, and shrubs grow, but larger plants cannot survive the cold.

The South Pole is colder than the North Pole because it is at the center of a mountainous continent, so the ocean does not warm it. The average temperature at the South Pole is -47° F (-44° C). Most of Antarctica is covered in ice all year round.

*Only the edges of Antarctica are bare of ice in summer. **Lichen** and mosses grow there.*

POLAR PEOPLES

Apart from **research stations**, Antarctica is **uninhabited**. Some peoples, such as the Inuit of Alaska, Canada, and Greenland, have made their home in the Arctic. The Inuit can teach you how to use limited **resources** to survive.

Building to Hunt

Today, only a few Inuit still live as hunters and fishers, keeping to their **traditional** way of life. They hunt for birds, fish, and **mammals**, such as whales, seals, walrus, polar bears, caribou, and musk oxen. It is impossible to plant crops in the icy ground, so they collect grasses, roots, berries, and seaweed. When hunting at sea, the Inuit travel in a single-person boat called a *qajaq*. It is made from a **driftwood** or whale-bone frame and covered in sealskin up to the paddler's waist, to keep it watertight and to let it be easily righted if **capsized**.

In winter, Inuit travel over the snowy ground and sea ice in sleds pulled by huskies. Sleds are made from bone, driftwood, or baleen, which is the tough, bristly plates from the mouths of whales such as the bowhead.

The Inuit bred huskies from wolves and dogs. They are strong, with thick fur to keep them warm.

Keeping Warm

Traditional Inuit clothes and boots are made from animal skins, such as caribou and seal, and sewn with thread from animal **sinew**. Arctic animals **evolved** to have thick fur, so their skins make warm clothes. Sometimes, the Inuit use the stomachs of whales and seals, which are waterproof, to make clothes.

During the winter, some Inuit hunters build **temporary** shelters out of snow called igloos. In the far north, some Inuit used to live in them all year round. Other groups once lived in tents made of driftwood or bones and animal skins, while others built homes out of the turf (the grass and layer of soil beneath).

FIERCE FACT!
When outsiders saw the smart design of Inuit boats, they copied them and adopted the Inuit name, *qajaq*, which became kayak.

Inuit coats, known as anoraks in the Kalaallisut Inuit language, have warm hoods lined with fur. This fisherman, photographed in 1929, has hunting weapons strapped to his qajaq.

POLAR SURVIVOR

In 1923, a Canadian expedition to uninhabited Wrangel Island, in the Arctic Ocean, ended in disaster. A 25-year-old Inuit woman named Ada Blackjack was left stranded.

Hostile Island

In 1921, the Canadians decided to claim Wrangel Island by starting a settlement there. Taking little more than tents, axes, and rifles, the expedition consisted of a Canadian man, three American men, and Ada, who was to cook and sew for them. Ada was a single mother who needed the money to pay for treatment for her son Bennett, who had **tuberculosis**. She had to leave him in an orphanage.

The men found it much harder to survive than expected. Realizing they would die from starvation, three of them set sail to get help in January 1923. They were never seen again. Ada stayed to take care of one of the Americans, Lorne Knight, who was sick. He died in June.

The temperature on Wrangel drops as low as -72° F (-58° C), so its landscape is bleak, icy tundra.

Learning to Survive

Ada had lived in the city of Nome, Alaska, and had no survival skills. She taught herself to set traps for Arctic foxes. She collected roots and birds' eggs. She chopped driftwood for fuel and collected snow to melt for drinking water. She sewed animal skins into warm clothes and boots. Ada had never held a rifle, but she carried one in case she met a polar bear. Gaining confidence, she built a lookout tower from driftwood. She then made a boat from driftwood and canvas so she could hunt seals.

In August 1923, a ship that was dropping off another expedition on Wrangel rescued Ada. She returned to her son and spent the money she had earned on his treatment.

Ada would have starved if she had not hunted bearded seals and other Arctic animals.

FIERCE FACT!
The last group of woolly mammoths survived on Wrangel Island until 2500–2000 BC, when they became extinct.

CHAPTER 2
WRAP UP WARM

Your challenge has begun. You find yourself alone on the ice, with no sign of life in any direction. You are colder than you have ever been. Did you choose the right clothing to survive this extreme climate?

Traditional Clothing

The Inuit and other Arctic peoples, such as the Nenets of Russia and the Sami of northern Europe, have made clothes and boots from animal skins, such as seal and caribou, for centuries. They recognize that the animals that survive in the Arctic have long, thick, **water-repellent** fur. Today, the hunting of seals and many other Arctic animals is banned or restricted to protect endangered **species**. Traditional peoples have the right to hunt some species for their own survival rather than for profit.

A Sami caribou herder uses his animals for fur, food, and transportation.

Modern Equipment

When explorers set off on polar expeditions in the nineteenth and early twentieth centuries, they dressed similarly to traditional peoples. Yet traditional peoples never went as far as the North Pole or set foot on Antarctica. The explorers found they had to wear many layers of wool, fur, and canvas, which were heavy and bulky. The natural **fibers** soaked up the explorers' sweat, so clothes froze solid overnight and were difficult to put on in the morning.

Today's polar explorers wear both natural fibers, such as feather padding, and man-made fibers specially developed for their useful properties. The underlayer of clothing is soft, warm, and **absorbs** sweat. The middle layer is **insulating**. It provides small pockets of air. Motionless air is a very good insulator because heat travels through it slowly. On the inside of this layer is a plastic film to prevent sweat from reaching the insulation. The outer layer is waterproof, often sewn from fabrics coated in a form of plastic.

An explorer wears snow goggles to protect his eyes from the sunlight reflecting off the snow.

BEWARE OF
FROSTBITIE

One of the greatest dangers you face is **frostbite**. It is most likely to affect your fingers, toes, and nose. Consider how you could modify your clothing to protect yourself.

Dangers of the Cold

Normal body temperature is around 98.6° F (37° C). If your body gets too cold, you could suffer from hypothermia. This is when your body temperature drops to below 95° F (35° C). The body can no longer warm itself, and so it starts to shut down. Early symptoms of hypothermia include severe shivering, fast breathing, and pale skin.

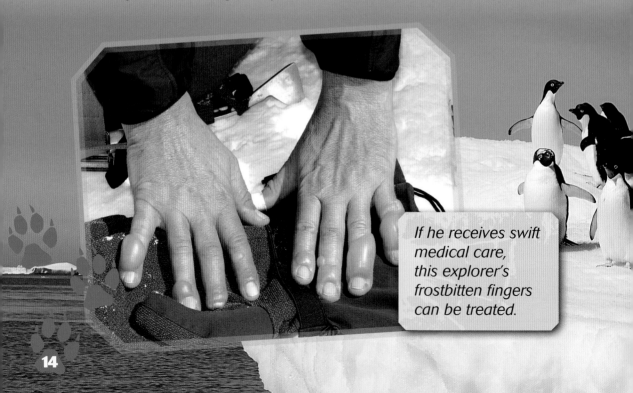

If he receives swift medical care, this explorer's frostbitten fingers can be treated.

Hypothermia often goes hand in hand with frostbite. Frostbite usually strikes the body's **extremities**. If your extremities get extremely cold, blood stops flowing to them, eventually damaging the skin and tissue. Symptoms include prickling skin, followed by numbness, then hard or waxy-looking skin. If you have frostbite or hypothermia, call for help, get into a warm shelter, and put frostbitten body parts in warm (not hot) water.

Maker Solutions

From the Inuit to sportswear designers, makers have come up with many solutions to the problem of frostbite. Balaclavas, or hats that cover parts of the face and neck, and padded gloves and boots can help. Mittens are better than gloves because they allow each finger to be warmed by the heat of the others. Boots should be waterproof. Socks can be made from a man-made fabric that absorbs sweat from the skin and seals the moisture behind a waterproof layer, sort of like in a baby's diaper. Heated foot pads and gloves use batteries, gels heated in a microwave oven, or **chemical reactions** to produce heat. Mittens should be pulled over the ends of sleeves and waterproof leg coverings pulled over the tops of boots. Finally, loops of cord can be attached to zippers, so that they can be undone without having to take off mittens.

FIERCE FACT!

Some animals that survive in cold conditions, such as whales, seals, and penguins, have an extra-thick layer of fat, called blubber, for insulation.

Adélie penguins have waterproof feathers and a thick layer of fat to keep them warm.

EAR TO EAR

If you do not keep your ears warm, the cold and wind will make them painful, and they could develop frostbite. If you did not come well prepared, consider making yourself earmuffs.

Chester's Earmuffs

People living in cold environments have always used fur or cloth hats, wraps, and hoods to cover their ears. Earmuffs, designed only to warm the ears, were invented by 15-year-old Chester Greenwood in 1873. He came up with the idea while ice-skating in Farmington, Maine. Chester was allergic to wool, so as soon as he pulled his hat over his ears, they started to itch.

When he returned home, Chester asked his grandmother to sew circles of warm flannel and beaver fur onto a wire loop. He applied for a **patent**, giving him the sole right to manufacture and profit from his invention. In 1883, Chester opened a factory to make earmuffs. The factory eventually went on to produce 400,000 pairs of earmuffs a year.

Most of us have probably never wondered who invented earmuffs!

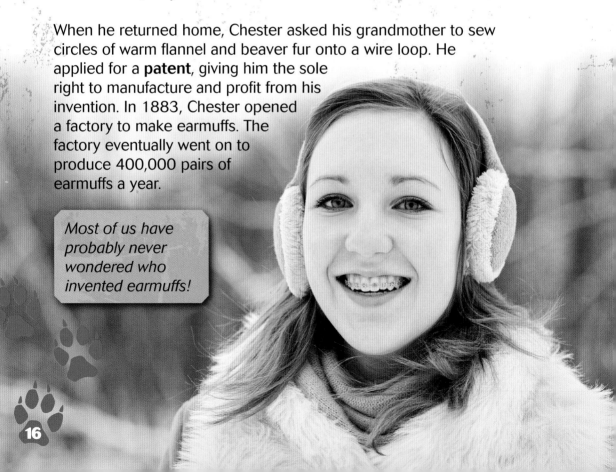

Make Earmuffs

From the supplies in your backpack, you will need to make:

→ Warm, soft pads to go over your ears
→ A headband to attach the pads.

Can You Make It?

Step 1
Consider which item from your backpack could form the outer fabric of your pads.

Step 2
Which items could be used to sew around the edges of your pads, leaving a 2-inch (5 cm) gap?

Step 3
Which item could fill the pads?

Step 4
Think about which tool could be used to attach your pads to your headband, then seal the open ends of the pads.

Headband

Pads

FIERCE FACT!
In Maine, Chester Greenwood Day is celebrated in December. A parade is held in Farmington, where people wear their earmuffs.

CHAPTER 3

TAKE SHELTER

Temperatures in Antarctica can drop as low as -128° F (-89° C). It is vital to have somewhere warm to spend the night or to take shelter from a blizzard. A shelter could be as basic as a bivouac bag or as permanent as a hut.

Bivouac Bag

A bivouac bag, called a bivvy for short, is a sleeping bag that can be used instead of a tent. Modern bivvy bags make use of man-made high-performance fabrics. They have a waterproof outer layer, with a special cover that zips over the user's face, while allowing him to breathe. They are thickly padded for insulation. Old-fashioned bivvy bags left the sleeper soaked with her own sweat, but modern bags use **breathable** fabrics. These fabrics have tiny holes that allow **evaporated** sweat, in the form of water vapor, to pass out of them but do not let large raindrops enter. A bivvy bag would keep you alive overnight if you could not get to shelter. What materials would you need to construct a bivvy bag?

This explorer in his bivvy bag may look uncomfortable, but he would survive a blizzard!

A Permanent Hut

In polar regions, there are few materials that can be used to build a permanent shelter. There are no trees on the ice or tundra to construct a framework. At the northern edges of Antarctica or on Arctic islands, a natural rock cave would offer protection from wind and snow. If you can see stones, animal bones, or driftwood washed up on the shore, these could form the framework for a hut. Some Inuit groups cut the top layer of grass and soil, using it to mold walls or roofs. Earth is good at keeping in heat.

FIERCE FACT!
The oldest buildings in Antarctica are two huts built on Cape Adare in 1899 by the explorers of the British Antarctic Expedition.

This turf-roofed Icelandic home has walls of stone to protect it from the wind and cold.

PITCH A TENT

Today's polar explorers take tents with layers of specially designed fabrics. The outer fabric is windproof and waterproof. The inner fabric traps heat but allows evaporated sweat to pass through. However, you need to build your own tent.

Weatherproof Shelter

For the outer layer of their tents, traditional Arctic peoples use animal skins, which when covered with fish oil or animal fat, become even more waterproof. Man-made fabrics that have been waterproofed with a waxy or plastic coating will perform the task even better. Water runs off the fabric rather than being absorbed by it.

Traditional peoples keep warm inside their tents with a fire or lamp and more layers of furs, blankets, and quilts. Air trapped between these layers adds insulation.

In 1964, the National Aeronautics and Space Administration (NASA) developed a material that is exceptionally good at trapping heat. It is a plastic sheet with a shiny metal surface that reflects heat. Often called a space blanket or emergency blanket, it is found in many first-aid kits to prevent hypothermia.

The Nenets people of Arctic Russia made these tents. The outer layer is caribou skin.

Make a Tent

From the supplies in your backpack, you will need to make:

→ A frame for your tent
→ An insulating inner layer
→ A waterproof outer layer.

Can You Make It?

Step 1

Consider which items from your backpack could form two upside-down Vs to make a frame for your tent.

Step 2

Which item could be tied between the upside-down Vs to form part of the roof?

Step 3

Which items could create the insulated floor and sides of your tent?

Step 4

Which item could form the waterproof outer layer of your tent? Consider how to make an air gap between your wall insulation and outer layer. Which local materials could weight it down so it does not blow away?

Waterproof outer layer

Roof

Insulation

Air gap

Frame

Local material to weight down the tent

SNOW CAVE

If you cannot find shelter and fear you are facing hypothermia, copy the polar bear and dig a snow den. Even if it is -40° F (-40° C) outside, it could be 32° F (0° C) in your cave. This difference in temperature might save your life.

Snow Insulation

Many animals, including Arctic foxes, Arctic lemmings, and pregnant polar bears, dig holes in the snow to keep warm during winter. Snow is a good insulator because a lot of air is trapped between the ice crystals. A principle to keep in mind is that warm air rises. For this reason, it is best to dig your cave into a slope, with the narrow entrance tunnel leading upward into the main chamber. When you are in the cave, heat from your body will be trapped inside.

The Arctic fox shelters in snow burrows during blizzards and extremely cold weather.

Start Digging

You will find it easiest to dig a cave with a shovel, even if it is cobbled together from items in your backpack. If you have to dig with your hands, it will take five or six hours to make even a tiny cave. The walls and roof of your cave should be at least 1 foot (30 cm) thick and packed hard so they hold their shape. The best design for the roof is domed, so that melting snow runs down the sides rather than onto your head. Although you need room to lie down, keep your cave small to keep heat trapped as close as possible.

Remember that being buried in a collapsed cave could be extremely dangerous. When your cave is constructed, consider piercing the roof or wall with a metal pole to provide a breathing hole in case it collapses.

Which items in your backpack could you use for digging?

INGENIOUS IGLOO

An igloo is a dome-shaped shelter built of snow. Traditionally, the Inuit groups of the far north built igloos. Just like the snow cave, the snow dome is an excellent insulator.

Build a Dome

To build your igloo, start with the dome. Find a patch of snow that has been packed hard by the wind. Cut the snow into blocks using a saw. Start by cutting large blocks, then make them gradually smaller. The hole left in the snow by cutting your blocks will serve as the **foundation** of your igloo. Using your largest blocks, place them in a circle. When you return to where you began, continue building, choosing blocks that are a little smaller than your previous row. Shape the blocks to tilt inward, with each block leaning firmly on those below. When you have completed your dome apart from the final, top block, choose one that is a little too large for the hole, then wedge it in. Pack loose snow over the joints between blocks.

A dome is a very strong structure. If someone stood on the roof of a well-constructed igloo, it would not collapse. All the blocks in the walls would support their weight equally.

Finishing Touches

Cut a few small holes in the walls and roof to allow fresh air in for you to breathe. At one side of the igloo, dig a short entrance tunnel, then cover it with blocks. This entrance will prevent heat loss when the inner door is opened. In a traditional igloo, the door is a flap of animal skin. The interior of the igloo is covered in skins, including beds carved from snow. The Inuit light an oil-burning lamp inside. The heat melts the insides of the walls a little. When they refreeze, they are joined together even more solidly.

FIERCE FACT!
The temperature in an Arctic igloo can be as high as 68° F (20° C), just from the warmth of the human bodies inside it.

An igloo's floor and its entrance tunnel are a little below ground level. This gives the structure extra insulation.

CHAPTER 4
FUEL UP

You have used up a lot of energy building your shelter. Even tramping through the snow is exhausting. You need to find food, and it should be packed with as many energy-giving **calories** as possible.

Few Animals

As Ada Blackjack's unlucky companions discovered, it is not easy to find enough food in the Arctic to keep up your energy levels. Traditional Arctic peoples are skilled at hunting the few animals that are found on the tundra, from caribou to birds, such as Arctic terns and snow geese. Along the shores and on the sea ice, traditional Inuit use their kayaks and **harpoons** to hunt for sea-dwelling mammals, which include harp seals, walrus, bowhead, and beluga whales. These mammals are covered in blubber to keep them warm, so the Inuit have a very high-fat diet, which also helps keep them warm.

The Inuit cut holes in the sea ice so they can dangle a line with a fake fish on the end. When a fish, such as an Arctic cod, comes to eat the bait, the fisher spears it.

On the shores of Antarctica, which are warmer than the frozen areas inland, you will find colonies of seabirds, such as emperor and king penguins, snow petrels, and snowy sheathbills. Leopard and crabeater seals rest on the ice offshore. Inland, you will not find an animal large enough to eat. A small, flightless **midge** called *Belgica antarctica* is the largest inland animal.

Like many Arctic animals, the walrus is endangered as a result of hunting for profit. Traditional peoples are allowed to kill small numbers to eat.

Frozen Food

When they are out hunting, the Inuit often eat meat and fish raw, right after catching it. Eating warm flesh helps warm up the hunters. Food may also be eaten frozen, which keeps it fresh. Back at home, food is cooked over a lamp of burning seal oil or whale blubber. On the treeless tundra, these are the only sources of fuel. The lamps, called *qulliq*, are often carved from soapstone.

GATHERING FOOD

You need to eat fresh fruits and vegetables to stay healthy. On the Arctic tundra, you will be able to find edible plants if you know where to look. In Antarctica, you will not be so lucky.

Arctic Plants

Along the shores of the Arctic Ocean, you can gather edible seaweeds. These can be boiled into a soup or stew over your stove. Throw in some other greens that you can pick inland, including grasses and fireweed, which has a reddish stem and dark pink flowers. Some plants store food in swollen underground stems and roots. Keep an eye out for spring beauty and sweet vetch. As many plants are poisonous, you should never gather food without the help of a knowledgeable adult.

Alternatively, let a tundra vole do all the hard work for you. Voles store small edible roots in their underground burrows. The Inuit raid these burrows. However, they always leave half the roots for the vole, as well as a small gift of food.

Be sure to leave a gift for the tundra vole if you steal from it.

Barren Antarctica

In Antarctica, 99 percent of the land is covered in snow and ice. On the remaining 1 percent, which mostly lies on the far north Antarctic Peninsula, you will find only two flowering plants: Antarctic pearlwort and hair grass. Neither is good to eat. During the summer, scientists in research stations get deliveries of fruit and vegetables from supply boats or planes. In winter, most scientists leave the continent, but a few members of staff stay through the dark, stormy months. No planes can deliver fresh food in the winter, so research stations have heated greenhouses where fresh vegetables are grown.

FIERCE FACT!

In Antarctica, scientists working outdoors take food that is easy to eat frozen, such as bars of chocolate and pemmican, which is a mush of protein and fat.

Cloudberries grow in the Arctic in temperatures as low as -40° F (-40° C). When ripe, the fruits are golden. Never pick a berry that has not been identified by an adult.

FOOD CACHES

The problem for explorers in Antarctica is to take enough food to get from the coast to the South Pole and back. It uses up vital energy to drag sleds loaded with food and fuel for cooking.

A Successful Solution

Roald Amundsen was the Norwegian leader of the expedition that first reached the South Pole, on December 14, 1911. Amundsen had a backup team of men who set up **caches**, or stores, of food and fuel along the early part of the route. The caches were buried in waterproof containers, with a line of flags marking the way to the food. The cold kept the food frozen and fresh. Some supplies were picked up on the way to the Pole, and some were reserved for the return journey.

There was another part to Amundsen's determined plan. Teams of dogs pulled his sleds. On the way back from the Pole, he killed some of the dogs, and he and his men ate them.

This photo was taken of Scott (center back) and his men at the South Pole in January 1912.

Disaster

Amundsen narrowly beat another team of explorers to the South Pole. English explorer Robert Falcon Scott and his four companions made it to the South Pole on January 17, 1912. On the way back, Scott's planning and his backup team failed him. They had failed to leave evenly spaced caches and did not arrive to meet him where they had planned. His stored fuel cans had leaked.

Scott could not bring himself to eat dogs, since he saw them as "friends and companions." His men pulled their sleds most of the way themselves. When a blizzard blew up, Scott and his men retreated to their tent, where they died from starvation and cold some time in March 1912.

FIERCE FACT!
When Scott saw Amundsen's flag at the South Pole, he wrote in his diary, "The worst has happened … Great God! This is an awful place."

Today, planes drop supplies for Antarctic explorers and workers. They are equipped with skis on their landing gear.

ICY DRINKS

There is a vast supply of drinking water in the snow and ice of polar regions. You simply have to melt it over your camping stove. But how will you stop the water from refreezing, so you can drink it while you hunt for food?

Thermos Bottle

Water freezes at 32° F (0° C), so to keep it liquid, you must keep it above that temperature. A thermos, also called a **vacuum** bottle, keeps liquids hotter or colder than their surroundings for a long time. James Dewar invented the vacuum bottle in 1892. It has an inner chamber for holding liquid. This is held inside an outer chamber. Between the two chambers is a gap, from which nearly all air has been sucked out, creating a vacuum. Heat travels even more slowly through a vacuum than through stationary air. This means that heat is slow to enter the bottle from outside, and a hot liquid in the inner chamber is slow to cool down.

You will not be able to create a vacuum without specialist equipment, but consider how you can slow down heat loss using insulating materials. Some materials are good insulators because they trap air between their fibers or in pockets. Air can also be trapped between layers of a material. Other materials reflect heat from their shiny surface.

A store-bought thermos bottle uses a vacuum to slow down heat loss.

Make a Thermos Bottle

From the supplies in your backpack, you will need to make:

→ A sealable container for holding melted snow
→ Layers of insulation to trap heat in your container.

Can You Make It?

Step 1
Consider which item from your backpack could contain melted snow.

Step 2
Which items could be used as layers of insulation? Choose another item to stick your materials together.

Step 3
Which item could be wrapped around the outside of your bottle to reflect heat back inside?

Step 4
Experiment with the different insulating materials in your backpack to see which keeps your water warm the longest.

Reflective surface

Container

Insulation

CHAPTER 5
MOVE ALONG

It is not easy to walk over slippery ice or through thick drifts of snow. Consider what footwear would allow you to make the best progress: skis or snowshoes? What materials could you use to make them?

Snowshoeing

When it comes to traveling over snow, look for inspiration from animals that make their home in the snow. The snowshoe hare's large hind feet do not sink into snow because their size spreads the hare's weight over a larger area. Snowshoes work on this same principle.

Traditional Inuit make snowshoes from animal bone and sinew. They are attached to ordinary animal skin boots. The snowshoes are sometimes triangular and sometimes circular, and up to 18 inches (46 cm) long. They have an open web to prevent snow building up on their surface, which would make them heavy. Modern snowshoes are made of strong, lightweight metals and plastics.

The snowshoe hare's hind feet are extremely wide. Their soles are also thickly furred to protect them from the cold.

Skiing Along

If you are pulling a heavy sled behind you, or you will be traveling a long distance, skis will allow you to move faster and with less effort than snowshoes. When Roald Amundsen traveled to the South Pole, his men used skis. These let them slide over the snow's surface, balancing themselves on ski poles with pointed ends. Their skis were carved from hickory wood, and the tips were upturned to prevent them from getting wedged into the snow.

Many of today's Antarctic travelers use skis that are shorter and wider than the skis used by sportspeople for speeding downhill. This shape makes them easier to maneuver. The skis also have grips on the underside, sometimes provided by a nylon skin.

FIERCE FACT!
In winter when snow is on the ground, the pads on a caribou's feet shrink. This bares the rim of the hoof, which cuts into the snow to keep it from slipping.

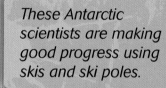
These Antarctic scientists are making good progress using skis and ski poles.

ON THIN ICE

Sea ice is frozen ocean water. It forms on the surface of the ocean around the North Pole and the shores of Antarctica. It is essential that you know the dangers of sea ice and whether it is safe to cross.

Freezing Over

Sea ice is different from icebergs, which are chunks of freshwater ice that form on land and drift off into the oceans. Saltwater freezes at a lower temperature than freshwater. Sea ice forms on the ocean surface when the sea temperature falls below 28.8° F (-2° C). Sea ice is sometimes unmoving because it is frozen fast to the land or the seabed. Other sea ice is free to drift with the wind and water **currents**.

Cracking Ice

Sea ice can be up to 15 feet (5 m) thick, which might make it stable to walk on. However, thinner sea ice may crack under your weight and tip you into the freezing water. Alternatively, you could step onto drifting ice that takes you out to sea. Poke a pole or animal bone into the ice to see if it is firm. Look for signs of seals on the ice, such as tracks or feces. If there are seals around, they must have come up through cracks, which may be hidden by fallen snow.

These explorers are examining an iceberg from the safety of a kayak.

Since no test is foolproof, make it a rule to stay away from frozen stretches of water. The Inuit used to know when sea ice was safe to cross, and they drove their dogsleds on long journeys across it. Today, global warming is melting the sea ice earlier in the spring and making it thinner throughout the winter. As a result, even experienced Inuit sometimes misjudge the safety of the ice.

A polar bear can survive a walk on drifting sea ice, but you probably would not.

FIERCE FACT!
The world's largest iceberg was called B-15. It was 183 miles (295 km) long. It drifted out to sea and broke into smaller pieces.

SLIDING SLEDS

If your backpack and food supplies are heavy, consider building yourself a sled to drag behind you over the ice. By not having to lift the weight above the ground, you reduce the amount of energy it takes to move it.

Hauling Power

If you haul your own sled, you will need to consume extra calories to make up for the energy you lose. If you do not want to haul it yourself, you must consider your choice of animal power. You will need a light sled and a large enough number of animals to split the effort between them, so that they are not exhausted.

It is important to choose animals that are at home in and well **adapted** to the polar environment. For example, if you chose horses to pull your sled, they would need warm coats and special snowshoes. The Nenets of Siberia use caribou to pull their sleds. The Inuit use wide-pawed, thick-furred huskies.

Dogsled racing is a popular sport in mountainous and northern regions. The dogs enjoy the race and are well looked after.

Sled Design

When designing your sled, bear in mind how friction will affect it. Friction is the force that slows down an object as it moves against another object or material. Friction can work both for and against you. Ridged soles on your shoes create friction that prevents you from falling over on ice, but ridged runners on a sled will keep it from sliding. However, if you make your runners too smooth, it will wriggle all over the ice and could endanger your animals.

The Inuit made their runners with upturned tips, carved from materials such as bone or wood, in regions where wood was available. Today, sleds are made of smooth and lightweight man-made materials, such as **carbon fiber** and **Kevlar**. These materials are strong enough not to break when the sled bangs into ice or rock.

FIERCE FACT!
Modern Antarctic explorers take sleds with solar panels, which give them power to use their laptops, linked to the Internet by satellite.

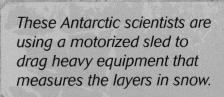

These Antarctic scientists are using a motorized sled to drag heavy equipment that measures the layers in snow.

CHAPTER 6

POLAR PERILS

It is time to find your way to safety. The longer you stay where you are, the greater your chance of being caught in a fierce storm, being attacked by a polar bear, or giving in to despair.

Conquer Your Fear

Alone in the polar regions, one of the greatest dangers you face is your own fear. Far from other people, you have no one to offer support or help you battle against hostile nature. Traditional Arctic peoples have had many generations to adapt themselves to the environment. They have the support of family and friends, as well as songs, stories, and festivals.

Scientists who work in Antarctica must go through many tests to make sure they are physically and mentally tough enough. Those who stay at their stations over winter face the hardest tests, since there will be several stormy weeks when no plane can land if someone is so homesick that they want to leave.

The Neumayer III Antarctic research station is on stilts so it is not buried by drifting snow.

In the Arctic and Antarctic Circles, you may see a light display known as the Northern or Southern Lights. It is caused by particles of energy from the sun colliding with Earth's atmosphere.

Dark and Light

In summer, seeing the bright sky at midnight can be confusing and exhausting. In winter, the total darkness lasts many weeks or months, depending on distance to the Pole. The human body needs sunlight to function properly. It allows our bodies to make vitamin D, which helps us take in **calcium** from our food. Sunlight also helps our bodies make **hormones** called melatonin and serotonin. These control our moods, sleep, and appetite. Without enough of them, humans can feel sad. In Antarctic research stations, every bed has a special light that mimics sunlight. On winter mornings, it gradually turns on, as if the sun is rising. In summer, thick window blinds allow a good night's sleep.

PREDATORY
POLAR BEARS

In Antarctica, there are no large land animals to do you any harm. In the Arctic, meat eaters include wolverines, wolves, foxes, and polar bears. Of these, only the polar bear is large and aggressive enough to be a real danger to humans.

Bear Habits

Polar bears are born on land, but they spend most of their lives on the sea ice, hunting for seals that come up for air at cracks in the ice. In summer, when the ice melts, the bears move inland to eat berries and any animals they can find, from birds to musk oxen. A hungry bear will attack humans. Male bears are up to 10 feet (3 m) long and have 42 sharp, jagged teeth. They are stealth hunters, which means the victim is usually unaware of the danger until an attack is underway.

Early Warning

When sleeping in your tent or igloo, it is vital that you rig up a bear warning system. If a bear enters your camp, it will trigger the alarm, giving you a chance to protect yourself. Store-bought systems have a tripwire attached to battery-powered bells or buzzers. You will have to construct your own tripwire.

Polar bears can smell prey from 1 mile (2 km) away.

Make a Bear Tripwire

From the supplies in your backpack, you will need to make:

→ A tripwire to surround your camp

→ Noisemakers suspended from the wire that will ring out if it is shaken.

Can You Make It?

Step 1
Consider which item from your backpack could be used as a tripwire.

Step 2
Which items in your backpack could be suspended from the tripwire as a noisemaker?

Step 3
Which other items in your backpack could be put into these containers to make a noise if shaken?

Step 4
Which items in your backpack could the tripwire be wrapped around to create a fence? You may need to make notches in these items to prevent the wire from slipping.

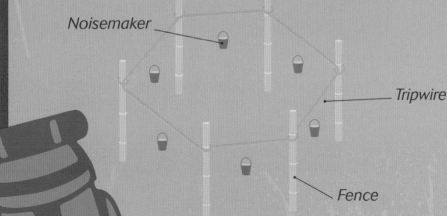

Noisemaker

Tripwire

Fence

WHITEOUT

Keep watch for gathering clouds and rising winds. Fierce snowstorms can descend suddenly. With winds up to 200 miles per hour (320 km/h) on Antarctica, blizzards can soon become whiteouts.

Blinded

A whiteout is when windblown snow keeps you from seeing more than a few feet ahead. During a whiteout, it is easy to walk into hazards, such as cliffs or cracking sea ice. As a storm blows up, try to reach shelter, and make a note of where dangers lie. If you are caught in the open, stay still.

You Survived!

As a whiteout descends, you crawl into a bivvy bag made from the emergency blankets and tarp in your backpack. When the wind starts to die down, you hear a strange roar. You peak out from your tarp to see three snowmobiles racing across the snow. You wave your shiny emergency blankets until the snowmobiles turn in your direction. The scientists who are driving them take you to their research station to wait for the next supply plane.

Three scientists are heading your way. Your ordeal is over!

ANSWERS—
DID YOU MAKE IT?

Did your makerspace survival skills pass the test? Did you select the best equipment for each "Make It Out Alive" activity? Check your choices against the answers below.

Page 17 Earmuffs
Thread • Fake fur, 20 x 20 inches (50 x 50 cm) • Plastic headband • Polyester fiber stuffing • Sewing needle • Glue gun • Pair of scissors
Cut two pairs of fur circles for the pads. Put the furry sides together. Sew with the needle and thread almost all the way around the edges of each pair of pads. Turn the pads inside out before filling them with stuffing. Use the glue gun to attach the headband to the insides of the pads. Seal the pads closed.

Page 21 Tent
• 2 emergency blankets • 4 metal poles, each 4 feet (1 m) long • Cord, 7 feet (2 m) long • Inflatable mattress • Tarp, 10 x 10 feet (3 x 3 m)
To make the frame, drive the poles into the ground, forming two upside-down Vs 6 feet (2 m) apart. Tie the cord between the poles to form the roof. The inflatable mattress and one blanket could form the floor. The other blanket could be draped over the cord to form the sides. For the outer layer, lay the tarp over the poles, leaving a gap between it and the blanket. Weight it down with snow.

Page 33 Thermos Bottle
Aluminum foil • Cotton balls • Paper towels • Plastic bottle • Plastic bubble wrap • Tape
Use the bottle for the container. Fill it with melted snow. To insulate it, wrap it in layers of cotton balls, paper towels, or bubble wrap. Wrap foil around the outside.

Page 43 Bear Tripwire
6 garden stakes • 6 metal buckets Marbles • Wire, 200 feet (61 m) long
Use the wire as the tripwire. Hang buckets filled with marbles on the wire for the noisemakers. For the fence, wrap the tripwire around the garden stakes.

GLOSSARY

absorbs Soaks up or draws in.

adapted When the features of an animal's body, or of its behavior, have changed to help it survive.

breathable Allowing sweat to evaporate.

caches Hidden stores.

calcium A mineral the body needs for building healthy bones.

calories Units of heat energy in food.

capsized Overturned in water.

carbon fiber Strong, lightweight man-made fiber used, for example, in aircraft.

chemical reactions When two or more substances combine to form new substances, often giving off heat.

currents Continuous movements of ocean water in one direction.

driftwood Pieces of wood floating at sea or washed ashore.

edible Safe to eat.

evaporated Turned from a liquid into a gas.

evolved Gradually changed over time.

extremities Furthest parts of the body, such as hands and feet.

fibers Thin threads of animal, plant, or man-made material.

foundation The weight-bearing part of a building below ground level.

frostbite Injury to body tissues caused by extreme cold.

harpoons Long weapons used especially for hunting large fish or whales

hemisphere Half of Earth when it is divided in two by the equator.

hormones Chemicals made in the body.

insulating Preventing heat from going out of, or into, something; still air is a good insulator.

Kevlar Extremely strong man-made fiber used, for example, in bulletproof vests.

latitude Measure of the distance north or south of the equator.

lichen A simple organism that grows on rocks, trees, or walls.

mammals Animals that give birth to live young and feed them with milk.

midge A small fly.

patent The exclusive right granted by a government to an inventor to make or profit from an invention for a certain amount of time.

phenomenon A fact or circumstance, often an extraordinary one.

predators Animals that kill or eat other animals.

research stations Places where scientists live and work.

resources Materials that can be put to use.

settlement A village, town, or other community of people.

sinew Tough body tissue connecting muscle to bone.

species A group of similar living things that can breed with each other.

temporary Lasting for a limited time.

traditional How things have been done for a long time.

tuberculosis An infectious disease that often affects the lungs.

tundra Treeless region in which the lower level of soil is always frozen.

uninhabited With no people living in it.

vacuum A space empty of matter.

water-repellent Not easily absorbing water.

FURTHER READING

Books

Cooke, Tim. *The Exploration of the North and South Poles* (Explorers Discovering the World). New York, NY: Gareth Stevens, 2013.

Martin, Danielle and Alisha Panjwani. *Start Making: A Guide to Engaging Young People in Maker Activities*. San Fransico, CA: Maker Media, 2016.

Sandler, Martin W. *The Impossible Rescue: The True Story of an Amazing Arctic Adventure*. Somerville, MA: Candlewick, 2014.

Taylor, Barbara. *Arctic and Antarctic* (Eyewitness). New York, NY: Dorling Kindersley, 2012.

Websites

Due to the changing nature of Internet links, PowerKids Press has developed an online list of websites related to the subject of this book. This site is updated regularly. Please use this link to access the list: **www.powerkidslinks.com/ms/arctic**

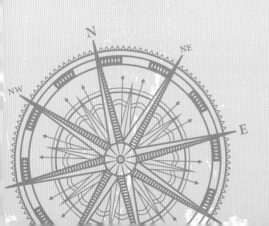

INDEX